MISTAKES ARE GREAT!

BLOOMSBURY EDUCATION
Bloomsbury Publishing Plc
50 Bedford Square, London WC1B 3DP, UK
Bloomsbury Publishing Ireland Limited
29 Earlsfort Terrace, Dublin 2, D02 AY28, Ireland

BLOOMSBURY, BLOOMSBURY EDUCATION and the Diana logo are trademarks of Bloomsbury Publishing Plc

First published in Great Britain, 2026 by Bloomsbury Publishing Plc
Text copyright © Matt Bawler, 2026
Illustrations copyright © Gizem Gözde Uçar, 2026
Matt Bawler has asserted his right under the Copyright, Designs and Patents Act, 1988, to be identified as Author of this work

All rights reserved. No part of this publication may be: i) reproduced or transmitted in any form, electronic or mechanical, including photocopying, recording or by means of any information storage or retrieval system without prior permission in writing from the publishers; or ii) used or reproduced in any way for the training, development or operation of artificial intelligence (AI) technologies, including generative AI technologies. The rights holders expressly reserve this publication from the text and data mining exception as per Article 4(3) of the Digital Single Market Directive (EU) 2019/790

A catalogue record for this book is available from the British Library

ISBN: PB: 978-1-80199-807-9; ePub: 978-1-80199-806-2
2 4 6 8 10 9 7 5 3 1

Printed and bound in China by C&C Offset Printing Co., Ltd., Shenzhen, Guangdong

To find out more about our authors and books visit www.bloomsbury.com and sign up for our newsletters
For product safety related questions contact productsafety@bloomsbury.com

MISTAKES ARE GREAT!

BLOOMSBURY EDUCATION
LONDON OXFORD NEW YORK NEW DELHI SYDNEY

From Kiev to Kampala...
From Turin to Tokyo,
there's a story that is spreading fast.

Have you heard it?

Do you know?

It's a tale that's hairy and scary,
of creatures who make giants quake,
that love to **ROAR** and gobble you whole,
if **EVER** you make a **MISTAKE.**

I wonder if I should stop right here?
Maybe it's too much to show.
I'll warn you now, you'll need to be brave...

Last chance...

OK then...

Here we go...

The legend of...
THE MISTAKE MONSTERS!

Our story begins in the lunch hall
at a school in the city, where Sue
was telling her friends of **MONS-TERRIBLE** ends
that could happen to me... and to YOU!

Get things WRONG
and you're GONE!

Eesa was painting a picture,
a portrait of Pedro his cat,
when his arm caught the side of the table,
launching splodges of paint with a **SPLAT!**

Eesa tried hard not to panic,
but his eyes began to stare,
for something blue was now stirring,
and **GROWING** right under the chair!

yikes! Oh no!
What could this be?
Is it something coming for **ME?**
It's got big eyes,
it's covered in fur,
run for your life it's a...

MISTAKE MONSTER!

Tallulah, who loved to invent things,
was wiring her robot to **ROAR**
but instead of a noise it breathed fire,
which burnt a **HUGE** hole in the floor!

Tallulah tried hard not to panic
but her cheeks were glowing deep red,
for something bright orange was stirring
and growing right under her bed...!

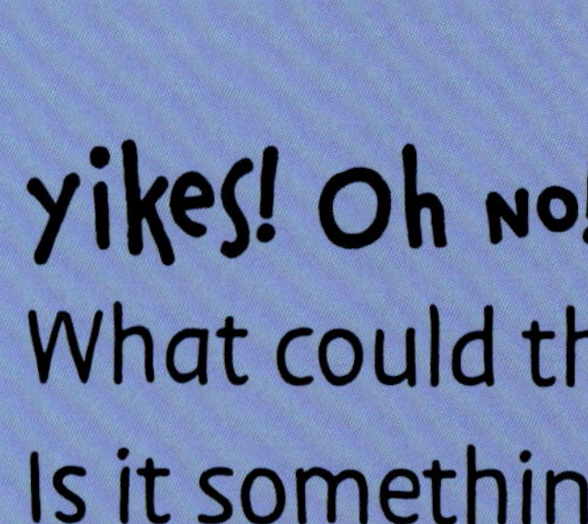

What could this be?
Is it something coming for me?
It's got big eyes, it's covered in fur,
run for your life it's a...

Max the magician was ready
to finish his show with a **'Wow!'**
He tried to pull a rabbit from out of his hat
but instead what came out was a cow!

Max tried hard not to panic
but his heart was starting to race,
for something pink was stirring
and growing right out of his case...!

Yikes! Oh no!
What could this be?
Is it something coming for me?
It's got big eyes, it's covered in fur,
run for your life it's a...

Naimah, who really loved dancing,
was trying to learn a new spin
when one foot tripped over the other
and launched her right into a bin!

Naimah tried hard not to panic,
but already she could see
that something yellow was stirring
and growing behind the tree!

yikes! Oh no!
What could this be?
Is it something coming for me?
It's got big eyes...it's covered in fur...
run for your life it's a **MISTAKE MONS...WAAAHH!**

Naimah was all set to scarper
but something inside made her stay.
She stepped a bit closer, then bravely she asked
'Mistake Monster... are you **OK**?'

Everyone RUNS when they see us
but there's no need to panic or yelp.
We're really not here to GOBBLE you up,
We come with a present to help!

Mistakes are **NOT** bad or dangerous.
It's very important you know,
that every time you make a mistake
it's a **gift** that can help you to **GROW**!

The friends paired up with their monsters
who gave their gifts with pride.
'What can we learn from these mistakes?
Let's take a look inside!'

Eesa **JUMPED** back to his painting.

Tallulah **RETURNED** to her bot.

Max **WHIZZED** off to his magic hat,

and Naimah **TWIRLED** back to her spot.

The Mistake Monsters gave them a boost
encouraging each child to explore.
They bounced back to taking big risks again.
Mistakes helped them grow even more!

Like stepping stones to the future,
our friends learned a secret that day,
Mistakes are part of the journey,
each time we make one, we pause and say...

MISTAKES ARE GREAT!

With smiles the monsters came over,
it was time to say goodbye.
'Don't worry', they said. 'We'll be back soon.'
'But next time, don't run, just say hi!'

Always remember...
Whenever you're facing a challenge,
'Getting it wrong' just helps you to grow.
Mistakes are the things that give you your wings
to reach where you want to go.

So now you've heard the full story
and the important message inside.
The next time YOU make a **MONSTER MISTAKE**
I wonder what YOU will decide?

Will you scream and run off in a panic?
Or be brave and decide to stay?
Look inside for what you can find
to rocket you on your way!

MISTAKES ARE

GREAT!

WELCOME TO...

THE COURAGE CLUB

This story is part of **The Courage Club** series – helping children (and their adults!) build bravery, take risks, and go after hard things together.

The bigger picture

So much of our approach to mental health is reactive: we wait until there's a problem before stepping in to 'fix' it. At *The Courage Club* we believe in a more proactive approach - one that supports ALL children to build strong emotional foundations right from the start. This is not just to equip children with the tools to cope when life's challenges come but also to empower them with the skills to thrive well beyond that.

The Courage Club is built around three core strands of child development:

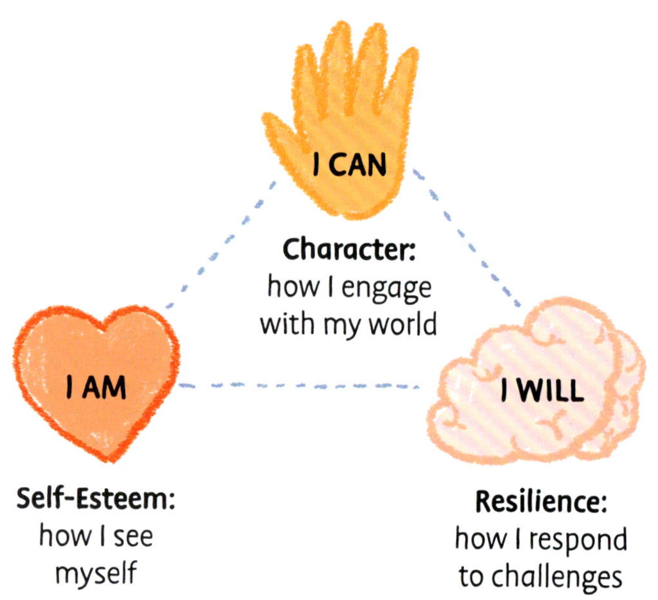

Where this story fits

Mistakes are Great! helps children see that mistakes aren't big, scary monsters to fear but powerful, friendly helpers on our journey of learning. Mistakes are how we learn best. Like stepping stones or a treasure map, mistakes show us the way and lead us to the gold. Have you ever felt the pressure to get something right straight away? Did that feeling encourage you to step forward or back? By normalising mistakes and celebrating each one as a brilliant chance to learn and grow, we remove the fear that often holds children back. When children see adults respond calmly, even joyfully, to mistakes, they learn to do the same.

So, let's keep saying it out loud, together: